Xmas 1944

To Mary LaperTragg
From
"Bob Lee".

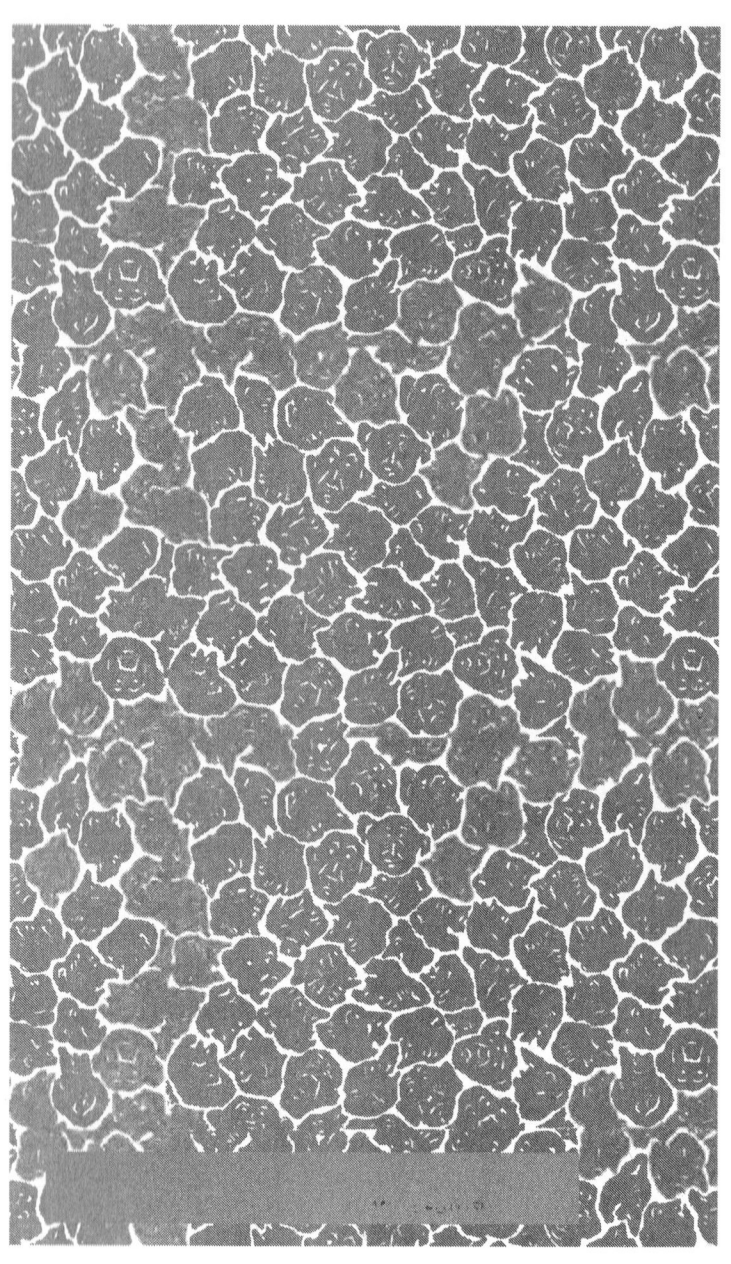

Copyright, 1884, by
Charles Scribner's Sons

The·fatal·mistake···A·tale·of·a·cat· 15

The·rash·act············ 16

Suspicion· ············· 17

The·pang· ·············· 18

The·rush·through·the·hall····· 19

And·through·the·library······ 20

New·treatment·for·the·mumps··· 21

Likewise·for·the·gout········ 22

Into·the·Kitchen· ·	23
Down·the·cellar·stairs· · · · · · · · · · · · · · · ·	24
{A·study·in·high·perspective·}	
And·out·into·the·cold·cold·world· · · · · · · ·	25
Carrying·everything·before·him· · · · · · · · ·	26
To·a·watery·grave· · · · · · · · · · · · · · · · · · ·	27
Ye·Aesthete·ye·Boy·and·ye·Bullfrog·	35
Ye·aesthete·readeth·Rossetti·to·himself·in·ye·garden·	36
Ye·sordid·boy·doth·"lam"·ye·tuneful·bullfrog· · · ·	37
Whereat·ye·aesthete·waxeth·mad·&·giveth·chase	38
And·pursueth·ye·boy·with·determination· · ·	39
Ye·final·heat· ·	40
Retribution· ·	41

The Balloonists

The start 51

Throw out some ballast . 52

Which causes some surprise . 53

Result of ballast throwing in bulk . 54

They throw out the anchor which catches 55

Back to Mother Earth . 56

Compensation for damages asked . 57

The Power of the Human Eye

The idea strikes him	73
He puts it into practice	74
And fails	75
Tries again with marked success	76
Again he tries	77
And again he fails	78
And yet again	79
Encouragment	80
He tries big game	81
And fails once more	82

The Arab boy and his elephant ***** 28

The old man of Moriches ***** 29

The bald headed man ***** 30

The mule and the crackers ***** 31

The influence of kindness ***** 32

Bobby and the little green apples ***** 33

The awful cornet	34
Tug of war	42
The fishermans lament	43
Rocketed cows	44
The grabful crab	45
Too much confidence	46
Illusory riches	47
The tooth carpenter	48
Science and force	49
The dynamite fiend	50

The last old man	58
The moth	59
The rover and the girls	60
The hornets nest	61
The unprogressive one	62
The flyer	63
Lo and the poet	64
The "left" Cow Boy	65
The too combative calf	66
The inquisitive patient	67
The bold Kangaroo	68

The truly good young man	69
The shark fisher	70
The high note	71
"Maria"	72
The unmusical anaconda	83
The bear hunter	84
The telescopic leg	85
The active "nusses"	86
The cat that thought it had a pudding	87
The slider	88

The sneezer 89
The ironical flamingo . . . 90
The idiot and the bull dog 91
Ye Ancient Mariner . . 92

The Fatal Mistake

A Tale of a Cat

Said this Arab boy Really now why
Should my elephant share in my pie
And the quadruped thought
It was time he was taught
So proceeded to knock him sky high

There·was·an·old·chap·in·Moriches·
Who·put·patches·of·tin·on·his·breeches·
When·asked·why·this·was·
He·replied·"Oh·because·
There·pretty·sides·which·it·saves·stitches·"

This man with a shiny bald head
Took his paper and quietly read.
Till a bee with a sting
At his scalp took a fling.
When he said things much better unsaid.

"Dear me," Quoth this mule, whats that crack?
'Twas a cracker the first of a pack.
 Since the second and third
 And the others were heard.
The critter has never come back.

This man in an amateur way
Went to taming a monkey one day.
"It is kindness," said he,
"That subdues it, you see."
But they didn't perceive it they say.

There was a musician from Brette
And all night he would play the cornet
The boarders they stood
All they possibly could
But one morning he left there you bet.

Ye Aesthete Ye Boy & Ye Bullfrog

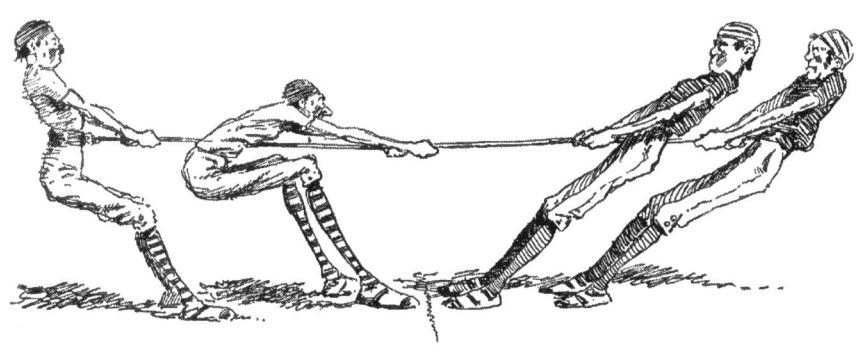

Tug of war is a beautiful game,
With a highly belligerent name,
But be careful to take
A rope that wont break
If you ever indulge in the same.

There was an old codger who said
"Quite enough of this hard life I've led.
As it's nearly high tide
I'll commit suicide.
I'll be far better off when I'm dead!"

Said this boy I propose to arouse
Those picturesque pasturing cows
Ah! wont they look fine
As these rockets of mine
Career through the spot where they browse

"This professor selected a crab
And observed "You will notice it grab
At you or at me."
They replied "Yes we see.
O! my! It's a regular dab"

This gentleman made a display
Of his talented parrot one day
"It bites others," said he
"But it never bites me."
But the bird alas! gave him away.

There was an old chap in Bay Shore,
And he said "Of red gold I've a store."
But it turned out alas!
That his gold was all brass,
And would not keep the wolf from the door.

Said this old "coon" who hailed from Duluth
To the Dentist who looked at his tooth.
"If you'll take it away
Quite handsome I'll pay."
It was done: but 'twas greivous in sooth.

7
This ruffian deadly and gruff
Thought the "old un" would drop quick enough
But the scientist read
From what science has said
And completly demolished the rough

This dynamite fiend to prepare
His explosive took requisite care.
But neglecting to get
The thing properly set
He received I'm afraid a bad scare.

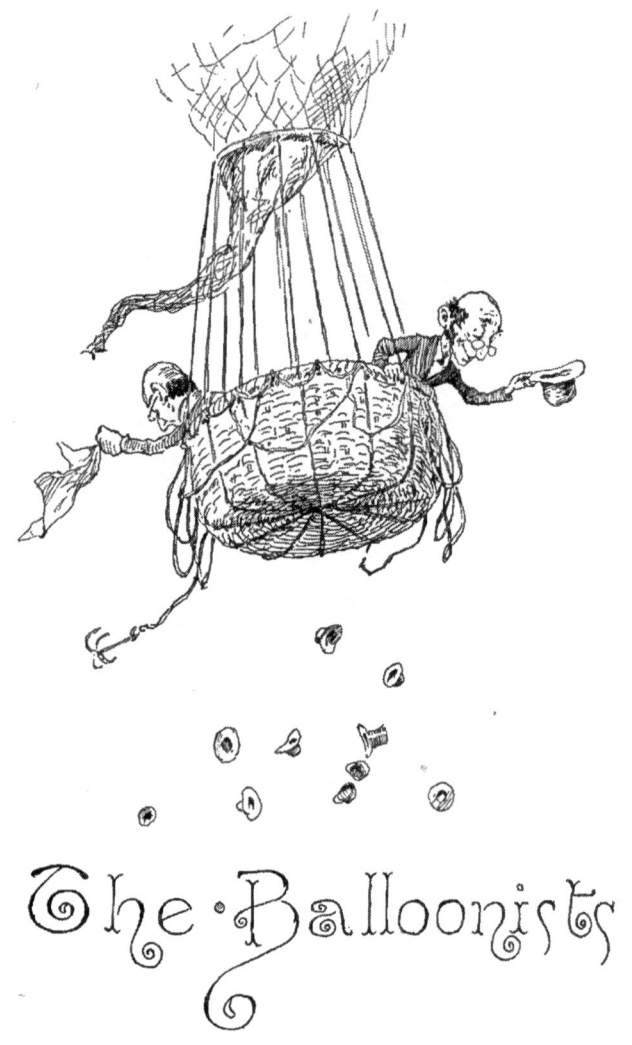

The Balloonists

There was an old daddy in Troy
Who said "I'm no longer a boy,
But I'll bet I can show
You chaps how to go,"
Which he did to his own savage joy.

In·it's·zigzag·mysterious·flight·
A·moth·is·not·easy·to·smite·
This·gent·thought·he·could·bring·
One·down·on·the·wing·
But·his·views·were·erroneous·Quite·

Said this person who hails from Glen Cove
"As the beach is quite empty I'll rove."
He hadn't gone far
When his unlucky star
Ran him into young girls quite a drove:

Said this duffer "My dear let us see
What that curious ball there can be
Why its hornets I swear
Of yourself love take care
This umbrella will answer for me."

Said this little black darky "O my
If I only had wings and could fly,
On dat wall I would get
And de peaches I'd get."
He flew, but he flew most too high.

This poet supposed if he gave
His works to an indian brave
The red man would melt
With the joy that he felt
The poet alas fills the grave

"Now hang me this wild Cow Boy" said
"I'll rush in and paint the Town red"
But alas for his plan
He encountered a man
Who buried him........'cause he was dead:

This old lady said "Johnnie come here
And water the caffy my dear."
The calf was untied
And to lead him John tried,
But it gave him some trouble we fear.

Said this man, "While I wait, I will see
What this curious object can be."
He went back with a yell
When the curtained thing fell
And since has not seen an M.D.

This remarkably large Kangaroo
Saw his chance to escape from the Zoo.
He took it you bet.
(Or he'd been in there yet.)
And he then through the multitude flew.

There was a young man in Montclair
Who said "I've that freedom from care
{Let it be understood}
Comes to only the good
For I neither smoke, drink, chew nor swear."

This fisherman said "What a lark.
I will bait and will angle for shark.
They pull it is true.
'Tis a fact that they do"
And they quite verified the remark.

The wolf of this shepherd boy said.
"I will quiet him now till he's dead."
But a high note occured.
And when it was heard
The wolf dropped the subject and fled.

There was an old cat named Maria,
Who to sing to high C did aspire.
In the midst of her wails
Came of water two pails,
Which had previously been near the fire.

The · Power · of · the · Human · Eye ·

He reads an article in a newspaper on the power which some people possess of quelling the most savage beasts by simply looking them steadily in the eye. He is convinced he possesses that power and resolves to make experiments.

He tries it on his wife.

When he regains consciousness it strikes him he must have failed; "possibly it was because I only used <u>one</u> eye," he said.

His wife's pet terrier succumbs promptly and he feels more confident.

He tries it on the chambermaid—

With rather disheartening results.

The parrot does not seem to yield as it might, either—

—but the cook's small boy shows most encouraging results.

He determines to make a great effort and seeks big game, he puts forth all his power—

—but, alas, fails once more.

This musical man thought that he
Had a seat on the stump of a tree.
He performed in a way,
That could move one they say
But the tree could move too, as you see.

There was a young man from Broadstairs
Who went out one day to hunt bears.
He found them indeed,
But it made his heart bleed,
For he came on them quite unawares.

Quoth this tramp with the Bowie "O ho
For that old snoozer there I'll lay low."
But the time honored Dick
Like a cyclone could kick
And the tramp never got any show:

These · nurses · could · never · see · why ·
Their · prices · were · thought · to · be · high
When · invited · to · go ·
A · trifle · below ·
To · skip · was · their · only · reply ·

This tom cat exclaimed "O ho ho
For that pudding I'll quietly go"
He was grieved and surprised
When the dish all capsized
And so was the party below;

"This corpulent lunatic cried,
By gravy, I'm going to slide."
But he slipt and he fell
And his friends couldn't tell
Where he went to though vainly they tried;

Said this snuff-taking Turk "Why with ease
I can stifle the noisiest sneeze."
But at Mosque one sad day,
His control all gave way,
And he startled his friends on their knees:

There once was a tall red flamingo
Who said "By the great jumping Jingo
I've been in this clime
An uncommon long time
But I haven't yet mastered their lingo"

This old lunatic said "Now I trust
That the chain of that bull dog wont bust".
But when it gave way
He said "Bless me, good day
I dont want to leave but I must".

There was an old salt in Nantasket
Set sail for Siam in a basket.
When a thumping big shark
Swallowed him and his bark,
Was not that a fine burial casket?

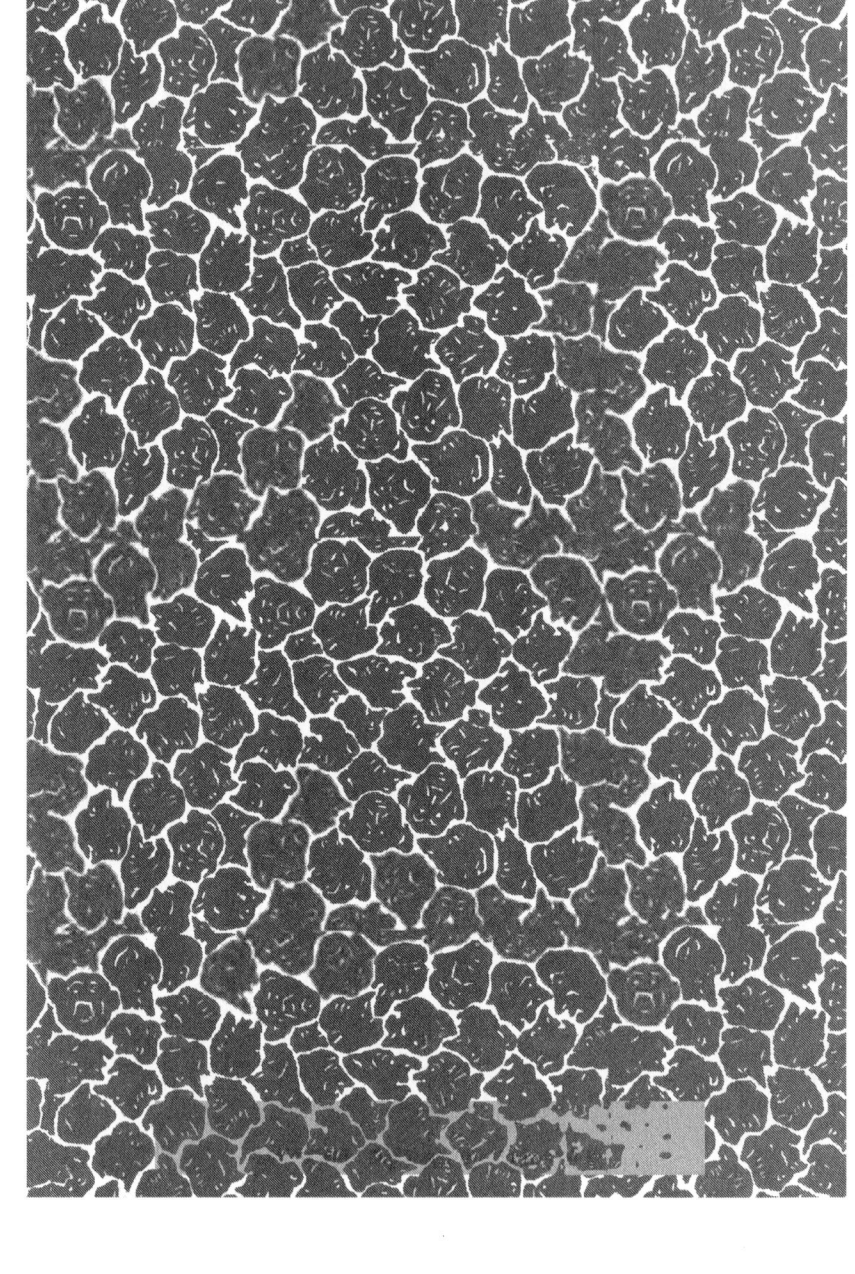

CPSIA information can be obtained
at www.ICGtesting.com
Printed in the USA
BVHW040912210721
612411BV00011B/3457

9 780344 977138